feeling and ugly

Published in Tshwane, South Africa,
by impepho press in 2018
impephopress.co.za
ISBN 978-0-6399465-1-1

Edited by Vangile Gantsho
Cover and layout by Tanya Pretorius
Proofread by Sarah Godsell

Print production by [•]squareDot Media
Printing by LawPrint

Earlier versions of some poems in this book have appeared in
the following websites, literary journals and anthologies: "Qunu
Poems," *The Johannesburg Salon* 8 (2014) • *Vanguard Magazine*
(2015) • "Of Love Letters and Other Gestures of Romantic
Love." *The Conversation* February (2017) • "Being/Becoming
and Undutiful Daughter: Teaching as a Practice of Freedom." in
Ruksana Osman and David Hornsby, ed. *Transforming Teaching
and Learning in Higher Education: Towards a Socially Just
Pedagogy in a Global South Context* (2017) • "a love letter in
five parts: A Response to Sara Ahmed's *Living a Feminist Life*."
Syndicate Symposia (2018)

feeling and ugly
danai mupotsa

acknowledgements

My father and I met for lunch the other day. As we talked, and laughed (because when we are together and we talk, I laugh deeply like I have met someone who knows me before language) I was suddenly full with that sense you get every once in a while that you are on a good path. When I think about my father and I, and our relationship, I usually remember just how much we cannot let something go until we feel the other one has fully heard us. We call each other stubborn. During this lunch, I was struck by how healing my relationship with my father has been for me in this life.

So my first thanks I extend to Isaac, my dad. Even where you have not understood, or agreed, you have never made me apologize for speaking. You are my teacher and healer in the practice of difficult love.

Eunice, Mama, you show me what it means to be a bad ass, complicated woman. You are generous and kind. Thank you for loving your difficult, complicated children so much.

Mudiwa, the gentlest soul.

Chenai, who brings so much light to us all.

Nyamikha, my only and most favourite daughter who has fire on her skin and poems in her heart.

In 2010, or 2011, or perhaps even 2012, Sarah Godsell invited me to sit on a panel as the 'gender expert'. Thandokuhle Mngqibisa performed and I felt this overwhelming proximity to feeling that I had put aside for a while. I wept. Thando, I am so grateful for you and your courage and your work. You brought me to proximity with myself and opened a door for me that I had closed tightly, imagining that I had neither the courage or the sense to actually live.

Sarah, you have called me a poet even while I could barely piece words together. You forgave me for drunken bus poetry. I am so grateful for your friendship. I am so grateful that your work is committed to poetry everywhere, refusing to slice yourself into parts.

Vangile, when I hear your voice (even when you are absent and I am reading your words on the page in my head) – I can feel myself move on the inside everywhere. It's like your words were sent to the earth to help me to remember to breathe.

Sarah, Vangi and Tanya, thank you for choosing me. and hearing me.

Thank you Quaz Roodt and SA Smythe, for hearing the poetry in me so long ago. Thank you Gabeba Baderoon for the same. Gcobani Qambela, Elliot James and Xavier Livermon for holding space on that bus.

I shared drafts of this work with many wonderful friends. Your laughter and crying and comments have brought this collection its life:

> Natasha Himmelman, Polo Moji, Dina Ligaga,
> Mapule Mohulatsi, Natasha Vally, Anzio Jacobs,
> Zuko Zikalala, Eddie Ombagi, Simamkele Dlakavu,
> Pumla Gqola, Elina Oinas, Zen Marie, Awino Okech,
> Farai Goromonzi, Miriam Maina, Sarah Chiumbu,
> Dorothee Kreutzfeldt, Charmika Wijesundara,
> Z'etoile Imma, David Kerr, Thobile Ndimande.
> I love you, thank you.

I am grateful for the space and holding at Jozi House of Poetry. Deep gratitude to Myesha Jenkins, Mthunzikazi Mbungwana, Rikky Minyuku, Khosi Xaba, Phillipaa Yaa Devilliers and Flow Wellington.

Thank you Lynda Spencer, Sharlene Khan, Thando Njovane, Yvette Abrahams, Neelika Jayawardene, Ranka Primorac for our time at Af-Fems.

Thank you Grace Musila and Hugo Canham for holding space as I shared this work at NEST. Thanks also to Peace Kiguwa and Shibu Motimele for the same.

Many thanks to Beth Vale for putting "If Pussy Could Talk" together, and Noizee Mngomezulu, Daniella Alyssa Bowler, Glow Mamii, Dinika Govender and Athambile Masola for sharing that stage.

Thanks to Ruksana Osman and David Hornsby for letting me include poetry in my chapter. Many thanks also to Panashe Chigumadzi and Thato Magano for publishing Recitatif. Thanks to Michelle Wolff for the Syndicate Symposia.

Love and light to the healers, my teachers: Lindy Dlamini, Sinethemba Makhanya, Matuba Mahlatjie, Sina Dondolo, Hashi Kenneth Tafira.

Mandaza Kandwemwa, thank you for seeing me, greeting me and all that gather inside and around me.

Thank you for your poetry and kindness Dhiren Borisa.

Lidudumalingani, thanks for reaching out and reading so closely.

I am a little terrified of going much further. There are important poets and writers who bring me life. I have the most incredible family and friends. I have colleagues who make space for me to bring the poetry to everything. I want to express my deep gratitude.

Thank you for reading.
Read me with all of the gentle.

foreword

Let me begin by confessing my sins to you, and then after, when I have laid bare my soul, I will continue to make my point. The storyteller in me cannot help but seek a narrative in every single poem. In poems that have traditionally constructed sentences, in poems that are written in sentences that seem to be incomplete, in poems that have no care for the laws of writing. The narrative is the way the poem lingers in my soul long after I have read it. It is how the poem leaves the poet's heart and into mine. My other sin is that I have no interest in text that turns me inside out. No writer should have the privilege of leaving me unravelled and in pieces that I fail to collect myself afterwards, I have always maintained. I do not want to spend days after reading a text feeling that I have been taken apart, that parts of me are missing and I am not sure where to look for them.

I read Dr Danai Mupotsa's poems over a period of two months, dipping in and out of them and yet returning to them always felt that the time I spend away from them was inconsequential. It is not the familiarity of the text that does this rather the poems extended themselves through me. It is a thing that can only be done with only a slight of hand, a thing that is not too deliberate and therefore not obvious. It is a thing that is not there, it cannot be pointed to, it cannot be underlined, it cannot be quoted, it can only be felt, even attempting to relay it betrays the intensity of the feeling it leaves one.

I think of everything in images and reading this collection, two visual references that are not related kept coming to me. One is an image of the unknown woman who had undressed into the nude in front of the Nelson Mandela statue in Sandton, South Africa, in 2014. The other is the 2007 film 'Awake'. In the film, the main character, a young billionaire, played by Hayden Christensen, undergoes a heart surgery but during it he has an anaesthesia awareness and hears the surgeons discussing a plot to kill him and collect the insurance money.

These two images conjure themselves up in my mind because of the feelings I had whilst reading this collection. A majority of the poems are deeply personal, about infidelity, sexuality, parenting, and reading them one can feel the depths that Danai has gone into to unearth her own feelings, ones that I imagine many of us would rather not, and then she goes to perform the act of writing these feelings into beautiful poems. Realising this, one begins to wonder how much this takes from one and how much it gives back.

Reading the poems also filled me with reluctance. I kept wondering if I should be reading this, if I am not being intrusive, but I remembered that the poet invited me, the reader, to read these poems and then I felt worse, because then I began to wonder if I had the aptitude to nurture what the poet had given me. The things we read nurture us but they too need to be nurtured in return. After each poem, its personal narrative, I felt like I was carrying Danai in thousand pieces of reflection and I had the responsibility, not so much of putting her together, but of carrying her with care, until she left me, and months later she has not.

…

by Lidudumalingani

Contents

mwana asingachemi anofira mumbereko

undutiful daughter

my father once said
he would not wish me
on anyone

he has lived a life of concern
for my teachers
friends
lovers
worried for them to meet me
without prior warning
or preparation

my father once said
he would not wish me
on anyone

shame,

he still stubbornly wishes
he could have raised
the stubborn
out of me.

little girl runs through the crowd
dances
like her feet are pulled to the sky
laughs gently

little girl plays with her friends
dips feet in the water
claps her hands with another
asks her questions

little girl catches the eye
opens her mouth even wider
stares close to the ground

little girl whispers

I've never seen someone so beautiful
looking so ugly,
he said.

He also once called me beautiful
he found me beautiful
and terrifying
and ordinary,
all at once.

So he kissed my face gentle
held my hand,
as though it might break him
then walked away.

feminist pedagogy

elaine salo taught me how to wash my panties.
she could see that I was trying hard not to listen
to my aunties
and my grannies
and my friends.
she saw their sadness
and their solidarity.
she told me hand wash only,
with Woolite
on a Sunday afternoon.
elaine salo showed me how to do this
just like my mother had once tried.
I made sure to try my hardest
to never wear panties
at all.
and we loved each other anyway.

little girls playing in a circle,
circle to hands
hands to hands
hands to claps
claps to smiles
smiles to skipping
skipping to laughter
laughter to flying
flying to moths.

little girls flying in circles,
circles to fingers
fingers to tips
tips to gentle
gentle to touch
touch to silken
silken like wings
wings like moths.

little girls with wings,
wings to fly
fly to touch
touch to finger
finger to play
play to circles
circles they fly in
they're flying like moths.

Wakes with praises for her mother
who raised her
with the knowing
of trees as kin.

The thing most interesting
about happiness is that its
machinations demand the containment of violence.

The face of beauty
recalls us
embraces us
endears us
warms us,
and love
contained in such extraordinary
   well perhaps just ordinary
violence.

I am a holder of faces

making love
means
sharing breath
means
rubbing bodies
means
wetness and smelling

I am a holder of faces,
collect them like fossils
so easily broken

I am a holder of faces,
like a stare down to capture all time and space
freeze them
seam them together,
so I might wake each morning the same

I am a holder of faces,
like I could gather you whole
from the base of the hand,
by my wrist

to the tops of my fingers,
like my aura would stretch from these fingers
through the archives you hold in your eyes

I am a holder of faces.

Recitatif/For My Daughter

Things my mother taught me:
never call a man
never ask him out
this is how you test your value,
women who fail to appropriately capture the attention of a
good, loving, committed
caring man
fail to know their value.

Things my mother showed me:
it is important to suppress
your rage.
unleash it in odd ways
manage it with wine
sad music
passive aggression
gossip
tears   to your children who
you expect to forget
how sad you were last
night, the next morning.

Things my mother made me feel about myself:
confusion
failure
deep desire for approval
confusion
failure
power in failure

standards   to living that
are not my own, but I use to prejudice myself
standards   to living that
can't possibly be her own, but

stand so powerfully
against us.

Ways my mother broke me:
attending only ever to
the ways I pleased her
on standards that break
women.

Never wanting to actually see me.

leaving

parts of myself
in my scratches
my notes
wishes and writing

parts of myself
at the doorsteps
of lovers,
equal parts
love and risk
equal parts fear,
imprints
on the face and hands of my daughter,
she is the teacher of compassion

letting myself die,
so that other parts of my soul might come to live.

cruel optimism

the belief that love will last.
the hope that justice is possible.
the wish for recognition.
the will to wake each day.

For the baby that I aborted

I miss you from places that my body cannot forget
I miss you from places my ancestors fail to find me
I mourn you from parts of my existence that only god can touch

I know survival,
it smells like your breath.

hardcore

I am hardcore like
sex in the backseat of your husband's car
while you are picking our kids up from school.
and I don't feel bad out it.
and I will deny it until the day I die.

Creamy soft serve
delicious.
Creamy soft serve
Delicious around the mouth
And sweet
Creamy soft serve
delicious
With softened crunch that
comes in the end
Delicious.

I'd run my fingers across your back
connecting dots,
playing gently against your skin.

I'd write letters
mostly in my head
sometimes spoken loud,
press my lips
and my breath
against you.

I'd lie next to you
and map our worlds together,
layers
one on top of the other

begging you
to love me.

On the rock

We stand
calmed still
for a moment of
engineered thought
and hot tears.

Some mornings I wake up and I just feel black
like I spent my nights dreaming fire,
each millimetre of my skin burning in a blue, red, orange, black
flame

perhaps it's easy to read me as familiar,
mummy, daddy
and black and brown girls and boys
trained in schools where only white women were our teachers,

you train me as your familiar
you don't know the girl who slept on the floor
that man huddled beside me,
I let him push his scabbed thumb into my body
made no fuss,
it was only a few hours
a place to sleep
and a job

at some seminar
I use words like discourse,
so you can see me
read me as familiar
you don't know the girl they took turns with
at that party   like a game,
they laughed.

You hear me use words like patriarchy,
wrap that p-word around my tongue
talk about it as a system, a structure, relation, an affect
You draw the distance between me
and all others   fog black

Love songs
freedom songs
fire songs,
are not always the same, you know.
It takes hard work to know the difference.
It takes hard work to learn other things.
Love songs
freedom songs

I want fire songs.

protest

gentle
wishing
drumming
screaming
broken bodies
singing

good wuk

little girls
and sad women
dancing
whining
while cooking in kitchens,
where dense pleasures
meet lessons
in friendship as violence.

little girls
and their aunties
dancing
whining
uncles pass
praise the cooking
and dancing
and whining.

little girls
learning to dance,
while laughing
and crying
and keeping quiet.

on the sexual division of labour

white people talk
black people dance.

please can I burn
some sage
all over
your mess

On Death and Pleasure

She wrapped her body
around her
like she might squeeze all life from her,
with all of her softness.

She looked at her eyes,
like deep inside them
were treasure maps
to war
or freedom.
To places where they could lean towards each other
completely
without fear of death.

She would lean into her
from behind
pressing her arms and hands and face against her,
pressing her tongue
rolling it in circles
and pushing inside her

blesser

sexy daddy
you hold me
in places
where I am
opening
squealing,
part boredom
part joyful
all shameless

fruit bowl

I want to climb you
like a fruit bowl,
awkwardly balancing
my fleshiest parts
against your hips
pressing your breasts
against my mouth
leaving so little oxygen
to share between us,
I want to climb you
like my friend Pumla rides
a fruit bowl
munching apples
like the deep hunger
inside her
will never cease
to need.

I saw you smile
and it was immediately apparent
that I would write love letters,
wishing for you
till the day that I die.

1. I want to make you happy

2. I love you

3. (Don't run away because of #2)

The come on

is me
hoping to catch your eye

is sometimes me noticing
you notice me

at the very end of the party
is sometimes my longing

sometimes yours
is your hand on my thigh

my hand accidentally against your chest
is two breaths caught in a kiss,

the come on
is all of our awkward

is me leaning my neck backwards
is your hand on top of mine
is our fingers connecting

the come on
is anticipating everything and nothing

the come on
fractures all of my sovereign

For the woman who had a baby with the love of my life

I will have to learn to love you
despite myself
and my heart
and longing

I will love that baby
like it grew out of my thumb,
and into the world to meet me

I will smile through my heartache
and watch you play your happy

I will try not to be petty

I will grow up

I will stop wishing that I didn't love him so much

I will learn to pretend
that he did not show me only indifference.

vampires

those uncles who teach us
to think
write
and breathe
from a distance.
while we cry for their recognition
numb in pain
and silence,
we lose the language
to speak
of how we
we are bled dry.

these uncles

ask us to be rational
while they rape us.

Dear revolutionary

My lips were woven together,
bits of emerald and mermaid
pressed together in p i n k, b l u e, g r e e n, p u r p l e l i g h t.
When the gods imagined my face
breathed words onto my tongue
caressed life into my feet, my stomach, my breasts,
they sang so loudly that my name would be heard by every other god,

yet you think I came here to be your healer?

How old is too old to still be sleeping with people's husbands at conferences?

jealous

watching you touch his hand
like you grew it in your own stomach
released it from your mouth
and kissed it
like you were born to kiss that hand,
turns me from the inside
like my body
might never forget
what it is like to want him.

wedding vows

I will love you until the day that I do not
It will be the kind of love that consumes
every part of you
When I am happy
you will know all of my happy
I will flood you with happy
and kindness
When I am angry
I will fill the room with all of my anger
I refuse to ever give you indifference
For as long as I love you
And I will love you until the day that I do not

Beloved,
you make me dream
only of nipples and
fingers and wet.

real friends know how to ride or die
at least that's what we promise,

watch them get married
and defend that ritual of lies
like that is the true friendship.

for the women who walk for so long each day
and every day
that they know no feeling at all
of exhaustion

whose bruises mark moments of collapse and return

whose mornings and evenings are stitched
so closely together
that their dreams have learned to slip through
the cracks of that darkness in bright, short, mostly shattering
flashes

who know no such thing as a time to be shattered

whose feet ache in the morning
when they wake to the next day
that first moment of breath
when they break with routine for the briefest awareness of the
body,
small ache in the lower back
and sharp needle across the side and the chest and the stomach

get up
feed others
lose tempers
speak sharply
speak softly
hold others gentle
keep walking.

my friends drink too much
they drink for happy
they drink for sad
they drink for bored
they drink for waking.
my friends all drink too much
like it pours into the parts of them where joy once lived
and we dance
we laugh
we touch
all the while.
my friends drink too much
like sadness is the place
where courage begins.

imphepho
(for Mirrie)

learning to love you came to me as fast and wild as breathing

I won't take a lover
who does not know what it means
to use their tongue.

when eyes to eyes

she let me fall,
let me fall off my social clumsy
let me drown

we would kiss
and hold
and strangle, gently

bar no sense from our play

and in the morning,
I would notice all the marks on her skin
place my fingers against each one
to see if it was real

it was like this for many days
love
bites
and drowning

I remember the first moment
that I noticed you
noticed your presence,
you hovered
like you loved the idea that no one noticed you at all.
I saw you move about the room
consuming it,
sight and sound
like you could be indifferent
until you noticed her
and in one moment,
it was all broken
one look could still slice you
right open

I noticed you
and loved you
right in that moment,
like I could collect your pieces
gather them in my hands,
crawl on my knees to rescue the smallest parts
use my tongue
and my tears
to nest you

despite all intuition to run
I turned to love, to rescue you
like a broken bird.

My whole life, I have loved you
broken bird,

my mother was a broken bird.

her mother found her
sitting on the floor
head leaning against the porcelain toilet
dead baby floating in the bowl
her mother called her a whore.
they never spoke of the matter again

Hilda

I

My grandmother is

a woman I never met.

she haunts.

her body seated next to me at night

hand presses against my face in my sleep

she brings the gifts of the water

begs me to jump into that pool

she rests in its depths

dreams the day I will join her.

II

You gave me the tools to piece myself back together.

III

I still feel your breath when I dream of walking past all of your
flowers.

rape trigger

It hurts so much
to be touched.

Like when fresh air hits you
in the lungs

and you choke,
chest feels broken

and you are hoping not to make sound.
It hurts so much
to be touched.

The Subject of "I"

For the shrieking spirits who sing through my spirit
and breathe through my stomach

I clutch desperately at bodies and smiling and kind eyes. For some sense coherence. Connection that means I have a place. I have no place. Words and tears pour hot, wet skin burns and feels like screaming. Face remains still mind retains control for a moment the cleverness suspends me in place where my voice speaks, does not break, and in the tone of silent scream speaks oneness of non-sense coherent incoherence.

I long for pleasure that comes with tongue and skin and eyes that touch and love on bottom and love on top softness and hardness and eyes. With self, and one and one and one; to feel your demand to possess every part of me as you try to clumsily collect me in those moments when I sit still and I just want to eat your face, your whole face and arms; consume you entirely for a moment suspended in the lies of affirmation. To only wake and remember my wounds, my incompleteness, my incoherence.

I want the spirits that course through my hot skin to refuse me, misrecognize me, hold me close and remind me of the control of love and the power of my wounds and that fire can never be still. I never want to accept or be still though I forgive my moments of stillness.

I want to live one and one and one
simultaneously
endlessly multiple
against all odds that I could ever escape one-in-three.

For witch, wizard, sage

My beloved,
who holds courage
where we are better occasioned
to silence
or comfort

My beloved,
who breathes kindness
into places where
others defend

My beloved,
who breathes smoke
into the parts of me
where my ancestors dream
that I might find them

My beloved,
part humble, part hubris
whose touch wraps around
my broken parts
and heals me.

I don't think that I will ever stop writing poems
about your face
and your voice
and your hair

I will write poems about your lips
and the way you hold your whole body
like it was the only ever body

I will write poems about the way that you use words
I will write poems like I'm hoping you'll notice
I will write poems about holding your parts and your wholes
I will dream of the touch between us

I sometimes forget what it means to know you in this world;
I don't know if I will ever stop writing poems about you.

I told her that I loved her
she told me "no thank you"
she said she could only offer me her broken,
must not have known
that I love her from my broken.

Dear heartbreak,
heartbroken
heartache

please find mop,
gather all of my tears.

show me yours, I'll show you mine

she asked me gently
to talk to her slowly,
because I found it difficult
to choose difficult
over resentment.

I told her I loved her
that's all.

she asked me again,
quite gently
to choose difficult.

I told her that I loved her
and
that it is difficult to tell her
that she hurts me with her indifference.

she talked to me slowly,
again gentle, almost like love
to choose difficult.

I stopped breathing
scared she might slice me open
in that moment,
closed my mouth
and chose resentment.

trigger warning

breathing
together like this
fills me with power.
breathing
together like this
fills me with pride.
breathing
together like this
hurts.
we breathe out of
the wound,
feels like breaking
into speech
into pieces.
breathing
together like this
fills me to pieces.

some people live in the most beautiful houses
there are beautiful gardens
graced with flowers,
the birds will visit in approval.
when you are invited into their houses
you will notice their happiness,
they show you in pictures on the wall
soft furnishings
gentle smells.
some people live in these most beautiful houses
where they never have sex.

Justice
is heartache
wrapped
in pretty paper
offered with
cheap sentiment
from friends
who own land.

Circus

Some of us grew up at Circus.
Our mothers left us with grandmothers
left us resting on slack bosoms,
while they learned pleasures
like dance and drink,
with our fathers
they drove home
drunk.

We snuck out the house
wore half-tops
and booty shorts
bought with stolen moneys
and borrowed fantasies.

At Circus,
We watched our friends pinned up against the wall
by boys our ages
and uncles older.
We snuck out of the bar with these men
who would touch us more privately
in the backseats of cars
behind corners.

Some of us grew up at Circus.
We would laugh
the next day
for friendship
about whose lips were cut from
too much passion
and too much force.
We would commiserate
for the one whose love never arrived.

I'm raging,
Sometimes that makes me petty.

I want to dream of love that is tempestuous
That doesn't come to me from behind
with badly formed cleverness and brokenness
That doesn't need to break my body,
this strange repetitive love that we learn to mean affirmation is
reciprocity framed by retribution.
No.
I want tempestuous love songs
that say only for now,
Because the second it feels like breaking
I am to find new home

they gather like smoke
first in small soft swirls,
and light-filled breath

they collect us
and all of our optimism
so, we dance for them
we dance,
like it might break the swelling in our feet
like if we dance,
we might ache less in our everywhere
like if we dance,
we might find pockets to place all of the kindness
that the world makes no space for

we look to the sky
bring salt to our tables,
we press our hands to the ground
we call on our senses
we pray for rain to come

Loathe the clever people
with no poetry
in their hearts

plant life

I would like to imagine
the kind of life
that allowed me a moment
of notice,
of cycles and promises
pockets of wishing floating dense in the air
taking in the promises,
like promises could ever offer even without a single touch

other times
I take time
to live
the kind of life
and notice,
mornings opening
with the embrace of large branches
kisses of blossom breath
and the weight of our dreams
collapsing together,
promises
memories
futures
collapse in a love affair
etched in the bark
and under my nails,
where we have climbed and crawled and held
where we have touched.

loving

takes courage

offers awkward pleasures
in waiting

demands
forms
of knowing

anticipates
aching

I can never leave the house
without earrings.
It's almost like
they hover over
the entire earth
carrying my body
shielding the soul-parts that rest in my stomach
from those
who might try to peer inside me

My earrings
hail storms
blocks of ice
crashing against the earth
they will break it
open for me
so that I can climb inside it
my blanket

My earrings
are made of smoke
and thunder
singing love songs
freedom songs
fire songs

I can never leave the house
without earrings

I mourn that sweet girl
that lives inside me.
She sits under a tree
and fears her own shadow.
She ran away from me
one day
because she saw all of my ugly
and blamed herself

I can only write love poems.

TITLES

red cotton by vangile gantsho
feeling & ugly by danai mupotsa

FORTHCOMING

Liquid Bones by Sarah Godsell
Surviving Loss by Busisiwe Mahlangu

Printed in the United States
By Bookmasters